A
Woman
Does It Better

A Woman Does It Better

A
Political Satire

from
A Future Woman President

as dictated to
A Very Lucky Lady

Website:
www.awomandoesitbetter.us
Email:
awomandoesitbetter@yahoo.com

ISBN 978-0-578-61794-7

CONTENTS

Before We Begin

LIKE MOST WRITERS I ASKED friends and relations to read this book before releasing it. Literally everyone who did so demanded more information about the First Woman President. More who, what, when, where, how and why. In short – her back story.

However, if you look carefully, you'll notice that the cover of this book does not say "written by" A Very Lucky Lady, rather "as dictated to" A Very Lucky Lady. I was simply granted the unique opportunity to put down on paper what the future First Woman President wanted to say.

Before getting this chance I had to sign a non-disclosure agreement from hell which, honestly, I didn't read that closely (does anyone?) so I don't know exactly how much I'd have to pay to whom by when if somehow something I released helped someone figure out the First Woman President's identity. Thus the question becomes: "What *can* I tell you?" The answer? Not too much, but I'll try.

I know her family tree is nothing super-special. Middle-class parents – one with a Masters, the other a PhD; one a math teacher and the other's PhD mostly underutilized. (Her dad even told me, "We don't really know where she came from. She's just driven.")

She definitely never expected to be a politician. She had earned a science PhD, on a full scholarship from a big BIG name science U in New York City. Her husband graduated from a BIG name law college. She and he were really your typical liberal New Yorker Yuppie brainiacs from what I have gleaned.

Until she had her epiphany. Though she never told me exactly when it happened I have my suspicions about the autumn of 2016. She did let slip that there was a moment when she thought "I could do better than that" after a woman did *not* become President.

What made her tenure so unique is her science and math background – analyzing raw data, reviewing comparative statistics, hard evidence, conclusions based on results – are her way of life.

She can out-read the best fortune tellers in divining the crazy tea leaves of US-economy statistics. And of course Social Media is basically in her DNA.

I don't know if she is Republican, Democrat, Libertarian or an "I Started My Own Party" person like President Macron of France. (It is *possible* for a US President to be elected through a write-in majority.)

She also understands "publish or perish" from obtaining her PhD. Her papers, book, blog, articles, comments on other's writings are what brought her national and international name recognition before she started campaigning.

Did I mention she has a genius IQ?

Hope you enjoy,
A Very Lucky Lady

From the Publisher

The First Woman President (F.W.P)
served two terms.

Written twenty years after she held office,
this abridged autobiography is being released now,
prior to taking place.

Maybe we can learn from history before it happens.

Historical Note

After iris scanning was legally accepted
as identity verification for driver's licenses,
passports and so much more,
anyone could securely log onto the Internet from
any computer anywhere via such a scan.

Elections (much less air travel)
have never been the same.

Introduction

I RAN MY CAMPAIGN ALMOST entirely over the Internet, resulting in my fancy words and "sound-bite" catch-phrases constantly being dehydrated down to a few letters or acronyms.

Even more humbling, many ideas were quickly reduced to condensed interpretations of what people thought I was *really* saying, and even those ideas were initialized. For example, a high-sounding, high-ideal campaign slogan like "less legislation, less government" was other-edited to "get rid of them," which soon degenerated to "grot."

Mutated to a verb, "grot" came to describe the intentional shrinking of any bureaucracy.

Today, the phrase "let's grot the place" connotes real people working out practical solutions – rejecting ungainly government intrusion.

Oh, to have introduced words like "aurora" or "finesse" into the language.

No such luck.

F.W.P.

I

How I Really Won

How did I become President? Well, I created a monster. Starting out as a simple idea, it quickly became as unmanageable as the evil villain in your worst-favorite horror film. In time, it infiltrated the world, oozing into every orifice and crevice.

The villain's name? Brazen Full Disclosure (or BFD, as the social-networking world shortened it).

The fundamental theory of BFD? Preempt any fear that one's deeply buried life secrets might be exhumed by self-exposing them, posting them on the Internet and linking to relevant documents. In other words, no secrets equals no lurid exposés equals no worries.

The Personal Data Proprietary Law established that only individuals themselves are legally permitted to release their own private information.

The controversies have been roaring ever since, including demands that certain information (especially concerning public figures) belonged in the public domain. Opposing howls from such officials that private information should be kept private were just as strong, but I thought, errant. After all, would a slave owner have voted for abolition?

I held that the way for an elected official to thwart misuse of private information was by self-exposing all such data, while at the same time requiring equal government transparency. An idea that initially alarmed conservatives as much as liberals.

Nobody said that starting a political reformation was easy.

I began by setting an example – hanging out my own dirty laundry in front of Village Earth right from the start. Every ugly little life secret became a matter of public record. Of course, that included sordid love-life details. Infamously, there was the older man whom I'd known biblically in college. This brief entanglement was evidenced by a hotel ledger sporting a false name. My marriage license, a public record, has my real signature. No handwriting expert needed to see that the scribbler of both were one and the same.

Then there was my driving record, including a too-recent country road 90-mile-an-hour Mustang outing.

My voting record, complete with holes and contradictions, was made public. As were memberships in Amnesty International, ADL, CAIR, People of Faith Network and the ACLJ. Then there was my expired membership in the ACLU. All out in the open.

Every tax return since my first. (Okay, so I didn't make a six-figure income doing mailings from home.)

Most relevant and important of all, I disclosed complete details of those who contributed to my campaign – names and amounts.

The American political establishment was appalled. Though not my intention, I had thrown down the gauntlet to every other candidate in the running. Any vote chaser who refused to disclose the full details of his or her contributors was seen, at worst, as crooked or minimally, untrustworthy. The electorate exercised their voting power accordingly.

Postings on the web, links to the details of campaign finances, yet more details. Not just names, corporate positions and incomes, but hyperlinks to balance sheets, Boards of Directors, each Board member's position on other Boards…

Wider and wider; deeper and deeper.

Starting as a chain of links, the details morphed into a web of interlaced documents spanning further than one could imagine. BFD became an infection that spread unfettered through corporations and governments alike.

Fund raising would never be the same.

Although my political opponents finally began to grasp the implications of BFD, they were too slow to embrace its full potential. I had out-danced them. So despite their expensive and not so clever attempts to sabotage my campaign, American voters were not fooled. How can you entrap a candidate who has no secrets? For a political establishment that saw elections in terms of who could bulldoze the most dirt on their opponents, I was a wild card.

My final opponent in the Presidential race used a televised debate to bring up that (now infamous) speeding ticket and memberships in "controversial" organizations. I laughed off the barb and dismissed the information as old news. Then followed up by challenging him to prove his claims to moral superiority by disclosing full details of *his* personal life. Left staring into the camera, eyes wide as those of a Hobbit caught in headlights, he would later admit it was at that moment he knew he'd committed political suicide.

I was elected to the White House by the largest landslide in history.

Of course, there is a downside to all this. Try explaining that a certain infamous underwear line is also super-comfortable when your shopping habits are out there for all to see.

HISTORICAL NOTE:
Claims of discrimination by politicians who refused to disclose their voting or driving records, much less any other personal information, were dismissed by the courts.

Judges kept asking the plaintiffs what they thought "public" servant means.

11

Why I Was the Most Popular President Who Has Ever Lived (So Far)

I CASTRATED THE IRS, IMPLEMENTED the National Sales Tax (Fair Tax) and brought an end to parasitic government – by using numbers, statistics, business metrics, graphs, pie charts, efficiency reviews – in short, concentraing on results.

This may not be completely true, but I get the credit for it.

The truth? The good-bye-IRS grassroots movement had been educating and popularizing this new hope for years. To be fair, I did have a few ideas that helped, for example, the National Sales Tax Elective (Yes, I know, NSTE – verbalized "nasty" – I actually liked it.)

The "nasty" part was easy. A repeating message of my campaign was my pledge to sign only laws granting greater freedoms. "NSTE" was the perfect appetizer for my taste. Anyone who wished to do so could elect out of Federal Income Tax and into "NSTE." It made more sense to have a flat rate national sales tax. (Don't even start with the "but the budget couldn't be balanced ..." malarkey. The costs to run the IRS, just the IRS, was over $12 billion, yes, b-i-l-l-i-o-n – per year.)

Within a year of passing NSTE, all sales taxable purchases conducted using plastic (by those opting in) were automatically set up to pay the National Sales Tax directly to the U.S. Government. (Paperless, paperless, paperless – an ugly, but popular, mantra.)

Of course, you can imagine what happened. Success was sweet. Thousands of jobs created, much less a whole new industry emerged to implement the system. All with private money, of course.

One side note: During my administration, the new measure of Presidential competence became the percentage of Americans employed in non-government jobs.

Convincing the banks about the Fair Tax was, not surprisingly, a more difficult task. They were looking at numbers that scared them. I had some real experts who took the loopy numbers, tied them in knots and then showed the banks how the dollars would really fall.

The approach taken? Let the marketplace decide.

Taxation would adopt a self-regulating, cross controlling new dimension. (Don't buy much, don't pay a lot of taxes!)

In the age of BFD, this was an easier task than we ever imagined. Government bureaucracies could no longer get funding without revealing how much, for what, to what result.

Every government contract, grant, endowment or funded project, became a matter not just of public record, but Internet dissection; which meant that real people – doing the work, earning the income, managing a household, raising kids, juggling two jobs and a mortgage – could see for themselves how some fat-cat politicians blew money away like dandelion puffballs.

This peaceful revolution made it easy to popularize statistical results as the standard measure of which programs were working, how much was being spent, and for what result. In fact, most of the stats were already calculated. The new angle was publishing them on the net for all to view, just like stock prices or currency exchange rates.

Probably as direct fallout, the term "professional politician" – PP – became something of a pejorative.

Legislative positions are almost exclusively held by volunteers these days. After all, who would want to listen to long-winded pontificating by someone who has never accomplished anything in the real world except getting themselves elected?

The end of politics as we knew it, catapulted my popularity.

HISTORICAL NOTE:

Ongoing criminal prosecutions of tax protesters faded into the sunset, just like the tax protesters themselves seemed to.

III

Being the World's Most Powerful Leader Is Easier Than You Think

---

WHY DID WE CREATE THE slogan "Better Ideas for Life?" By the time that phrase was coined, I was savvy enough to know that it would be reduced to its component initials. Fine. BIFL it was. I kind of liked it. But in the world of cruel masters the acronym BIFL didn't stick, instead quickly devolving to "The Big B."

Subsequently, in my administration, every idea had to pass the "Big B" test. There were "Big B" websites, heavily promoted by my Vice President, who as well as being the youngest man to hold that position, was also a talented techie.

How could Austin, Texas find out how Portland, Oregon tackled a problem Austin was running into? Easy. Go to a Big B website – categorized and cross-referenced by size of town or city, geographical features, type of difficulty, etc.

Big B websites had to include costs, results and statistics. Some say that the now accepted cultural requirement that naysayers and critics must come up with a better solution, rather than just fault-finding, began with Big B.

The Big B philosophy? Simple if innovative: If one is opposed to a proposal, come up with a brighter idea to solve the problem.

Better Ideas for Life encompassed:

- Better ideas for creating a 100% literate society.
- Better ideas for handling crime.
- Better ideas for increasing morality and personal ethics.
- Better ideas for preventing unwanted pregnancies thus circumventing many abortion delimmas.
- Better ideas to make a country with no illegal drug abuse.
- Better ideas for the more mundane but vital problems of food, clothing, transportation, housing and cost of living.

All of these ideas could be found on the Internet on Big B websites, most put into practice without much government intervention.

Another central philosophy of my administration was that if something is worth having, it is worth paying for. This led to highways being funded by gasoline tax, food inspectors being funded by food producers (After all, they have a vested interest in the excellence of all food products.) and national parks services converted to non-profit organizations, paid for by tax-deductible donations.

Thus evolved the Incredible Shrinking Government. (My nickname for this phenomenon – ISG – pronounced "Isgee" with a hard "g" – actually stuck for once.)

One of my first executive orders was to impose a moratorium on any new federal government hiring. That got the ISG meal simmering. Veto stamps branded into any Congressional salary increase proposal added a certain singed aroma.

It was obvious to me that if the government were a corporation, it would have quick-sanded into bankruptcy long before. My simple mission: create a lean, efficient and proactive federal government that served the people rather than ripping them off. Washington, Inc. became a PR firm, while other actually important activities – affordable health care, air traffic control, keeping international trade smooth and criminal-free – were divvied out into efficiently run publicly held corporations; the American people as shareholders.

Of course, flack arose from the deep-rooted D.C. establishment. But I had an overwhelming mandate from the American people. With stratospheric approval ratings (and I knew that if I appealed to good old "return on the dollar" common sense of my fellow Americans as well as to constitutionally correct Federal Government activities) I could overcome any political opposition.

Privatize, Privatize, Privatize. Another not so pretty mantra, but the melody lingers on.

HISTORICAL NOTE:

Rumors about why the original owners of the "Big B" website name dropped their copyright lawsuit were laid to rest when a former Big B model, now holding a highly paid job in a cosmetics firm, explained how she obtained her new position through executive talent alone.

IV

Much Ado About Nothing

Of course, my presidency had its fair share of infamy. As explained, I hired no new employees with federal funds. (Just for that alone, I could have been the most popular President ever.) I accepted no government salary, since I was doing fine from book royalties. (Thank you very much.) I worked from home. We converted one bedroom into a high-tech video/phone conferencing facility. I made few public speeches, instead doing most of my "talking" through the White House website. (Not utilizing 280 characters.)

I wheeled and dealed with leaders from all over the world on behalf of the American people. My favorite headline from Washington Speaks magazine was "She Walks, She Talks, She Negotiates."

My operating basis slowly sank in. Based on often repeated down to earth and easy to understand fundamentals:

- The President is NOT the most important person in your life … YOU are.
- More legislation is NOT the solution to all that is wrong with the world … ACTION is.

The White House became a tourist attraction, managed by the National Park Service. Scads of people willingly volunteered as:

- Official Presidential greeter
- Official Presidential hand-shaker
- Official Presidential letter-responder
- Official Presidential photogenic smiling face
- Official Presidential listener
- Official Presidential turner-over to someone whose job it actually is to deal with what you need help with
- and so many more.

The volunteers were badged, photographed and made "official." Once completing their three-month stint, they relinquished their duties to another.

I sauntered through the White House anonymously every once in a while.

All in all, everything ran pretty smoothly. Upstairs was Volunteer Organization Command Central (yes, VOCC, say that three times while trying to make it not sound vulgar), which had satellite offices in governor's mansions around the nation.

The Secret Service hated the new paradigm. As professionals at protection – who, what, when were they supposed to protect now? (For some, it took a while to understand how we were defeating security concerns. The answer was simple: If nobody is too important, then everybody matters. If no one location is crucial, then all can pulse with life.

HISTORICAL NOTE:

Complaints by architects of the Ronald Reagan Federal Building arguing that it was not intended to be an after-school arts and crafts facility for inner city youth and protesting the primary color interior design scheme backfired nicely.

V

Killing War

In the early 21st century, the following facts were true:

1. More and more of those involved in combat were mercenaries – "guns for hire."
2. The literacy level of countries where organized fatal conflict still occurred was abysmal.
3. Warmongers consistently fooled tiny pockets of humanity into believing violence was a viable option.
4. Worse, "educated" and industrialized nations profited from other-side-of-the-world conflicts, manufacturing and selling the guns, tanks, missiles and drones that enabled others to hold power by force and terror alone.

While not desiring to alter profitable occupations of humanity, I was determined to do something about the level of regional bloodshed.

Education was my weapon of choice, based on a simple hypothesis: that the advance troops of physical carnage are the propaganda and lies that justify murder, making the real battleground that of ideas.

I was determined to address a situation where so many people were ready to kill, driven by the conviction that others are either evil incarnate or will murder them first if they don't kill them first if they don't …

Entire nations were buried in twisted truths submerged by hate, covered with vengeance. Voices of remorse, forgiveness, justice and reconciliation were drowned out by the din of screams for death or revenge.

The best defense system against the cycle of violence was something that is impervious to any tool of destruction ever spawned. That something is knowledge.

A powerful army for peace – already in place, but thus far little utilized – included:

- The Infantry: millions of civilians sickened by the horrors of war but duped into believing they were powerless to end it.

- The Officers: teachers, already on the front lines in the theater of thought.
- The Special Forces: anyone with children, related to children or friends of children, including moms, dads, aunts, uncles, older brothers, grandparents, neighbors.
- The Supreme Command: A growing movement for non-violent change in place around the world and in touch through the Web.

The juggernaut of non-violent conviction created was called "Alter the Future" simply known as ALF. Properly armed, I hoped that it could stop war forever. A non-profit, education-endowment fund, ALF was powered up with three rules:

First: A full year's education for any child who so chose would be paid to go to any school, anywhere, plus clothing, living expenses, books, food, unlimited telephone calls, and regular visits home.

Second: Paid if the young person went to live with a family in a foreign country, as an exchange with a child from that country studying in the land of the first.

Third: Any ALF student who wanted to travel again in future years could do so. After staying in their home country for a year, they could go to a different nation, and to another family, up to the age of eighteen.

No expensive marketing campaign was needed; conscription for this militia of understanding was purely voluntary.

Planet Earth's peace hawks envisioned the potential with speed. A few hundred children mushroomed to thousands, and thousands to millions. As ALF gained momentum, so did the donations to its administrative fund. In most nations, those donations were made tax deductible.

And all of this was administered entirely over the Internet, with mirror websites in every country. Naturally, there were a few glitches at first, but they were smoothed out in record time.

ALF did not cost American taxpayers a dime. Airlines, hotel and restaurant chains made special arrangements to become official sponsors.

Proud of ALF's actions from day one, we were emboldened when virtually every US state, followed by country after country, set up local ALF organizations (ALF-CAL, ALF-France, etc.). ALF eliminated all the ballyhoo about school vouchers and enabled any person on earth to get a quality education.

Schools went back to teaching the three R's after soul-draining outcome-based, test-only oriented education programs were rejected as character destroying. Hyperactivity was found to get a swift kick when energetic children ran around on recess breaks every 2-3 hours. Funding for music, art, drama and many more programs was reinstated.

Major muscle was added as hundreds of endowment funds provided increasing bonuses for every year of ALF schooling completed. ALF students were able to graduate from high school, pick up a $50,000 graduation bonus check, and start life at the opposite end of the credit/debt snake pit.

By the end of my tenure, a large proportion of "higher" education was conducted over the Internet. Former liberal arts college campuses make wonderful artist communities and athletic training camps. Finally, former collegiate athletes (now well paid) made real money – not just their colleges and coaches.

Responding to the phenomenal impact of ALF, the United Nations proclaimed all international ALF children "Planet Earth Citizens" (PECs), and granted them special passports, carrying the right of unrestricted travel anywhere on earth, with the full protection of the United Nations. PECs became the targets of choice for global corporate headhunters.

Raised on the theory that every live human body is operated by a unique spiritual presence, thus deserving of mutual respect, PECs were direct in their actions to change the world. It was they who forced the conversion of stealth bomber factories into research and production facilities for high-speed and energy efficient civilian transport. A group of PECs also conducted a study to prove that former nuclear missile operators made excellent space flight traffic controllers. They had a major influence in eliminating all gender and race references on job applications.

These days it is hard to explain the concept of war. It gets slotted in with flat planet and chemical imbalance mythologies. There are still tensions in the world, but thanks to ALF we are much better equipped to address them and prevent them from flaring into armed reactions than at any earlier time in human history.

HISTORICAL NOTE:

It was never proved that there was any hanky-panky involved in the leaking of the Department of Education's (DOE) budget proposal (with salaries in the many multiples of teacher's salaries), which appeared in the mailboxes of PTA presidents all over the country. The ensuing implosion of the DOE did, however, make millions available for

improving schools (dictionaries for every
child, high speed Internet access, etc.).

Don't despair,
former federal employee
unemployment benefits
remain among the best in the world.

VI

Transparency as a Way of Life

THESE DAYS, NO ONE DREAMS of running for public office unless they can stand up to the scrutiny of Brazen Full Disclosure – the BFD standard. Gradually the BFD beast has swelled to affect much of the world. No serious investor will dip into anything that is not obviously actively BFD. Any legitimate corporation's stationery has the "BFD" logo neatly displayed; storefront windows all over the world display bright "BFD" stickers. On the Net, you can find BFD corporation's balance sheets, payroll details and contracts with countries worldwide.

The sea of information generated by BFD is not just deep, it is subterranean.

Certainly, there were groups who decried BFD. For example:

- Former "mental patient advocacy rights organizations" that were in fact funded by pharmaceutical companies.
- "Three-strikes" tough-law lobby groups who wished to obscure the financial contributions of penitentiary guard unions.
- "Women's Reproductive Rights" groups that cooperated with a profit-making abortion industry – while doing far too little to make free birth control available to those most vulnerable.
- "Anti-globalization" groups whose illegal methods and violent acts displayed the true level of interest in the less fortunate they claimed they were trying to help.

Nobody has mourned the demise of those groups.

Freedom of Information Act veterans from the trenches of the 70's cheered and editorialized, extolling BFD's virtues, while numerous repressive regimes hated the USA more than ever. Too bad for them. They tried to tighten the center, but the sand in their hourglasses kept plummeting.

All over the world, freedom was winning the fight against despotism.

Somehow, documents that could not be published inside certain borders became open to international scrutiny on US websites.

The Internet miniaturizes the planet so nicely, don't you think?

HISTORICAL NOTE:

Lawsuits filed in the World Court against the F.W.P.'s administration, claiming the sovereignty of other nations had been overridden by posting their state secrets on government websites, were unsuccessful. The failure of these suits led to the disclosure of even more top-secret dossiers.

Transparent does, after all, mean "see-through."

VII

An Affair With the Media

Being President presupposes interactions with the media. One does have control over the intimacy of that connection.

My media relationship might be best represented by the following interview, recently undertaken for this book:

"What do you think of Newstime's review of your book, Ms. President?"

"Newstime's review? Surely you mean Bill Bologna who works for Newstime?"

"Well, yes."

"Now, Bill Bologna. What has he published?"

"He's a critic. He does reviews."

"Oh, he gets paid for reading what other people have published and then saying what he thinks of their writing?"

"Yes, that is what a critic does."

"Has he ever written a book, a play, a short story or a movie screenplay himself?"

"No. Actually, maybe yes, but never gotten it published."

"Yet he gets paid to tell people what to think about other people's books, plays, etc.?"

"Well, he tells them his opinion."

"Now, isn't that an interesting job? And what are the qualifications for such?"

"He's written a lot of pieces about other people's writing, starting with smaller publications and working up to Newstime."

"So, the more critiques one writes, the more one gets to write them. Nothing to do with writing books oneself to get an understanding of what it actually takes to formulate an idea, start writing, keep on writing, creating people and scenarios out of thin air with only imagination to sustain you. Those aren't the people who make judgments about others?"

"It doesn't seem so."

"I can understand that. Those people are probably too busy working on their next book, play, etc."

"Yes, maybe."

"So, is that what most of the media does? Watch others living life and critique it? Don't they have to have done any of the things themselves that they talk about?

"Actually, no."

"But they speak so authoritatively."

"Yes, well, many of them have been doing their jobs for a long time."

"Oh, watching what other people do and writing about it?"

"Some of them talk about it on radio or TV too."

"Ah they're professional spectators. I guess they concentrate on sensational stuff because they find it exciting. Don't always have time to check out their 'facts' because there is so much going on. Sometimes even make things up because they'd rather be writing fiction."

"Uh..."

"Seems they could be using their skills as investigative journalists, digging into who is really behind worsening conditions in society. Exposing such. Making a difference."

"Certainly a thought."

"Yes, well, thank you. Fascinating. Looking forward to meeting more of those investigatory types."

Strangely enough, the discussion never got around to actually talking about Mr. Bologna's opinion of this book.

Another approach I quickly learned in dealing with the media was to get real; loudly asking personal questions myself, especially during a lull in the surrounding conversation. Questions such as:

"Tell me, Joe, when was the last time the woman you slept with didn't overact her satisfaction?"

"Excuse me, Sally, but are you really taking dangerous psychotropic medications which the FDA has warned can cause liver damage, mania, as well as homicidal and suicidal thoughts?"

I made it my business to keep up-to-date on the public information about a reporter's personal quirks, interests and habits.

We came to an understanding – stick to the issues.

I had some good takes on the real controversies too – might have helped.

HISTORICAL NOTE:

The "Enrich a Life" campaign for members of the media was a great success. Tutoring programs, mentoring and widely diverse community service activities resulted in significant tax write-offs.

VIII

Big Kids Play Rough

FORTUNATELY, LYNCHING HAS DROPPED OFF in popularity over the last hundred years or so. The donkeys and the elephants wanted my hide and couldn't decide whether to take the help offered to drag them into the 21st Century. By the time they made up their minds, it was too late.

They were antiquated – keeling left, veering right; giant ships with broken rudders floundering on public opinion, smashing and sinking on failed initiatives; incestuously gorging themselves and filling their favorite pork barrels while leaving most Americans hungry for real nutrition.

The real winners? The image spinners; video producers, companies who printed fliers, posters, and made fancy hats, convention organizers, so many more. All of them paid – no matter what the outcomes.

Effecting change in national politics was mostly a matter of making better use of Internet forums, encouraging voters to press forth with hard questions, providing statistics and solutions. Direct-to-voter referendums became an increasingly common way of effecting national policy. If Congress were deadlocked over a particular issue, the voters would be asked to make up their minds for them in the way of an online referendum.

We took the Article 1, Section Four phrase about Congress meeting "at least once in every year" seriously. Congress people now meet in person one day a year, treating it as something of a vacation, given that they now couple their congressional duties with real jobs. For the rest of the year, to satisfy tourists, mannequins fill the seats of the two chambers quite adequately.

HISTORICAL NOTE:

The requirement for anyone running for elected office to have held a position of public service, such as fireman, school teacher, librarian, scout leader, or policeman, was never actually passed into law. Still the range of day jobs that some of our congress people now hold are pretty amazing. Somehow these days a background as a lawyer is a big minus.

IX

Mars and Beyond

WHILE ALF WAS IN FAST-FORWARD relative to most government programs, it was in super-slow motion in other respects since the results would take multiples of years compared to the speed of high-powered rifle bullets, much less passenger jets converted to missiles.

We needed a "right now" fix.

Ending nation-against-nation aggression started with establishing public relations outposts around the planet and culminated with the first human base on Mars.

Eliminating the planetary drug scourge was a beneficial side-effect.

Maybe the most downright fun thing I got to do as Prez was reversing, thwarting, outwitting, outsmarting, and double-crossing the haters of ALF. It quickly became apparent to me that I needed some real pros on board, to establish PR outposts that would be fundamental to the success of ALF. It occurred to me that I needed people like the guys who saved the "New" Coca-Cola disaster; the folks who popularized bell-bottoms and wide-ties; and whiz kids who convinced people fancy coffee was worth the price of a frozen pizza. Peaceful resolution of regional tensions was a product, and it had to be marketed as such. If flavored water could be sold to the four corners of the Earth, surely we could sell peace and knowledge.

We started with surveys and opinion polls, crafted to determine what people thought they hated about America, what was being said, what was true, what lies, how we were making it worse, and how we could make it better.

With this information, we hoped to fix what was broken.

Most pleasurable of all, I personally got in on reviewing and tweaking localized strategies to change our activities, clarify our position, make the truth known, and circulate facts and figures to disprove some of the rumors.

It was a too-slow process, but I was determined to defy the cynics. We established open houses, conferences, associations geared towards cooperation and mutual assistance.

Meanwhile, law enforcement and intelligence agencies ferreted out the spreaders of lies, exposing their criminal pasts. This task was ideally suited to the covert operations guys, who had feared that the success of ALF would make them redundant.

Our next task was prosecuting real criminals according to the laws of the land and of the civilized world. To this end we used the World Court, and successfully battled to finally give it some teeth.

It became increasingly common to resolve international tensions by legal means. The chant "Criminal Trials, Not Missiles" became prevalent after its use in my first State of the Union address. Nice ring to it.

Concurrently, and reversing their historic role, the CIA was assigned to help make peace by exhuming, categorizing, indexing, codifying and simplifying the warehouses of information filed and stored on the violent and war mongering.

The documents were turned over to the PR types and spin-doctors to crystallize and interpret.

The findings were amazing, unbelievable, shocking and, in many cases, quite disturbing. I tried to imagine why people would commit such awful atrocities against others, and came to two conclusions:

In summary, those profiting from violence thought they would give themselves and their children a better future, by destroying the evil "others" who were responsible for everything bad. If the "others" were gone – the causes of evil – virtue would prevail. They were fighting the "good" fight, again and again, in scenario after scenario. They were "killing to survive by destroying evil."

OR

They were simply in it for the money. They didn't care who lived, who died, they were making money out of it. Lots and lots of money.

That they were also destroying their own ability to enjoy life and beauty was disregarded by those making the money selling the guns that supplied the armies that shot down the innocents.

It was a vicious circle. It was an intricate knot of violence that nobody had ever fully untangled. My administration could be the first. We ignored the protestations of special interest groups campaigning on behalf of arms manufacturers. I refused to meet with them.

Too often they were really the hidden voices speaking covertly to both sides and stirring the pot while staying out of the direct glare themselves. Of course, the Secret Service was alarmed by the fact I had made enemies of arms dealers and manufacturers around the world. But the will for a peaceful world was mightier than their bullets.

The PR men had a daunting job on their hands. Their usual big bucks had to be earned. Because this time they weren't selling a faster car, or a new brand of soda or even phones with the latest bling. They were selling the concept of peace. Instead of making profits for a major corporation, they were building a solid foundation for the future of all of Earth's children.

How to placate those employed by the defense industry? Millions of livelihoods are made that way; there are families to support, mortgages to pay. Those working in that world couldn't be cold-heartedly dumped onto the streets. They needed a better job. There was one out there.

Mars, ugly and mean, was waiting. Earth to space station; space station to Mars; something a whole planet could work together on achieving.

We had to start now, or I'd never see humans walking on Mars. (Why not provide more fodder to the no-moon-landing conspiracy theorists?)

Tremendous technology would have to be developed. Millions would be employed in a space project that made the 60's seem like building with tinker toys. The skill set of the defense industry was ideally suited to the task.

Getting the first International "Mars and Beyond" corporation set up was harder than it looked. We started by assembling representatives from the top international aerospace and defense companies.

After months of haggling, negotiating, bartering and arguing – a preliminary framework for the company was established. After that, the formation of international space exploration companies under the aegis of Mars and Beyond became much easier.

Convincing all nations of the civilized world to agree that any investments into these corporations should be tax-free was not an easy task. Tea with the Queen didn't quite cut it. Saki with the Japanese premiere was pleasant, but not quite enough. We had to offer major trade concessions to our partner nations to bring them to the negotiating table. In retrospect, it was a small price to pay. The talks earned me the title of "The Great Negotiator." I didn't mind.

Behind locked doors, a little inside information (another task for which the CIA proved useful) went a long way.

Which brings me back to tackling the drug problem. Once rid of terrorism, the world's attention turned to another group of murderers – the drug barons. We started by offering amnesties for those caught in the sell and consume web and assigning the cultivators and barons to agriculture projects on the bleak, unforgiving wastelands of the Red Planet.

Let's see what they can manage to grow up there (besides potatoes).

HISTORICAL NOTE:

Though most of the PR campaign to popularize the new space race was not controversial, the "Sex in Space – The Final Frontier" slogan maybe could have been thought through a little better.

X

Planetary U.S. Citizens

We didn't have time to wait for all the grade school kids to grow up before we dealt with the threat of nuclear war.

Why not open our borders to all the high-techies who were desperate to visit the US right now?

We created the U.S. Non-Citizen Passport (one of the "freedom" laws – laws that granted greater freedoms). USNCP holders were classified differently than Greencard holders, because of their special passports which afforded them the rights of both unlimited travel and U.S. residency as long as gainfully employed.

Their "benefits" would be tied directly to their contributions (by that time we had no income tax).

USNCP holders had to take one pledge; never to be involved in any aggression on U.S. citizens. Were they guilty of such a crime, they would lose their U.S. Non-Citizen benefits instantly.

HISTORICAL NOTE:

*Even with a down-sized air force,
we had to keep fighter jets
doing their air-show stints;
they inspired and impressed.*

*Aircraft carriers provide really
fantastic adventure vacations.*

XI

Educate Not Legislate

REFUSING TO PASS UNNECESSARY LAWS requires a converse – encouraging education and understanding. We started by slashing the salaries of legislators (dubbed "Bloodbath on the Beltway"). That move provided funds to instigate incentive programs for high school teachers – to attract the best and brightest. The result was a generation of bright, energetic 18-year-olds graduating highschool equipped to tackle the future.

There were those who didn't think it could be done. But my reasoning was simple: How many people's lives are directly impacted by the average high-school teacher in the course of a career? How many combined years of productivity do a teacher's students have in their futures?

Now, what about a legislator? Apart from passing laws and listening to self-interest groups, what else do they do? Do they *really* change anything? Or is change really effected by the hard work of people who bring issues to their attention?

Of course, it all came to a head with the matter which proved the true value of our legislators. An exposé revealed that in passing a bill to prevent their fellows from accepting soft money, the cost to the taxpayer – in man-hours alone – for passing the bill would have paid the college education of dozens of people.

Facts and figures started the slide of highly-paid lawmakers. All I did was increase the tilt.

Education became more than a matter of ABCs. It became a matter of how to do your own research, how to align your vocation to your passion and how to understand the studies yourself and dismiss interpretations done for you by political razzle-dazzlers.

HISTORICAL NOTE:

Fewer new federal laws were passed under the F.W.P. than any previous President. The story about fork-lift force required to obtain her legislative signature wasn't all that fanciful.

XII

International Neighborliness

ENTICE THE EXTENDED FAMILY OF a dictator to pop over for a quick visit. How about a week? Why not stay the summer? You can't all stay? Well, certainly some of you can. You'll be amazed at who you'll get to meet; extended families of the elected elite, nieces and nephews of the world's most rich and famous, grandchildren of czars. We're constantly entertaining people from around the world, all funded by a portion of what was formerly the U.S. defense budget.

Education? We have some of the finest schools in the world. Travel? The USA is a huge country. You could spend years traveling and still only see a fraction. Languages? We have people from everywhere who speak every language known to man. Arts? We have music, museums, opera and theater. We're open to cultural exchanges from the world over. Romance? We have wonderful people from all corners of the globe. Exchange visits? Certainly, members of thousands of our families would love to take extended visits to your country.

What? You heard that the adult children of leaders of hostile nations have accidentally met, fallen in love and wish to marry? Which might change the future of the world? You think this requires high-level mediation?

We'll be happy to accommodate.

HISTORICAL NOTE:

Papers filed in the International Court of Human Rights demanding "release" of family members were easily countered. Affidavits making clear how much they were enjoying their stay, much less photos and live video feeds to the court, proved there just weren't any valid causes of action.

XIII

Not So Neighborly

Did you say your country has been involved in funneling arms to terrorist groups and suddenly you just cannot get your products out of embargo at US ports? Your goods seem to get stuck in a no-man's land for months? Paperwork keeps disappearing?

Oh, your country has huge harvests, exportation and profits through the cultivation of certain flowering plant crops, the products made from which are illegal in most parts of the world. Somehow none of your college-age students can find a US school that will accept them? Can't get your people into important international technology jobs?

Goodness!

Yes, the President's Office and Department of State will look right into it. These are serious allegations and are going to require very deep study. Perhaps, just to help us in our investigations, you could make sure there is no truth to the rumors of profiting from death and get back to us.

Excellent. Good Idea.

Looking forward to hearing from you soon.

HISTORICAL NOTE:

That no terrorist organization actually ran munitions factories, much less could produce armored vehicles whereas China,Germany, Russia, South Korea, Hungary, The United Kingdom, France and others did, was easily pointed out as a major situation needing handling to free up pesky importation problems.

XIV

Separation of Church and State Does Not Mean Man Is an Animal

---

My passion for freedom energized me into public office. I refused to sign any law that I felt would diminish our freedoms but was enthusiastic about laws that increased freedoms. Signing bills such as the early voting law (pass a citizenship test and earn your voting rights), and the early work law (pass a literacy/capability test and earn your right to work and be paid just like the next guy) invigorated my presidency.

Yet my deeper passion was for freedom of conscience and belief. Not freedom *from* religion, rather freedom to have religion (or not) as one chooses. Not discrimination against atheism, rather recognition that atheists are being true to their own conscience. Judging people by deeds rather than thoughts.

I am a passionate advocate of the freedom to express all those things that religious conviction can bring to the world; compassion for one's fellow man, concern for a better life for all mankind, human rights and human dignity. All this made me in favor of more spirituality, not less.

It even made sense that if people believed they would be returning to planet Earth in the near future, they might act more responsibly today. Certainly a practical enough concept.

What if humankind is supposed to create heaven here on earth; if that is our responsibility? Certainly, there are a lot of people on the planet who look at life that way. Besides, what could it hurt to think that way? Floating around for eternity playing a harp could get boring pretty fast. After three days I would be craving chocolate chip cookies not to mention my conjugal rights.

I tell you this to document the mindset from which the criminal "justice" system as it was misnamed in the 21st century was attacked and destroyed.

With the same passion that I cherished America's freedoms, I detested people being stored in cages, out of sight, out of mind, ignored and forsaken, all for the sake of "justice."

I was further offended by the concept of abusing law-abiding citizens by making them work and pay to feed, clothe, house, medicate, placate, entertain and generally make penned-up people even more criminal.

Even worse, Americans had become accustomed to supporting an industry of "professionals" at keeping other people penned up; turning prison guards into soulless prisoners of their own consciences. A system that provided no hope and no future for either keepers or inmates.

This system was the product of a mankind that has risen to new heights of civilization? Seemed more like a society falsely convinced that men are no better than lions or tigers or bears.

We will not even broach the taboo subject of any society legally murdering one of its own due to an inability to rehabilitate the individual in question.

I was sickened by the knowledge that most of those incarcerated could not read, rarely had a father in the home, had almost never held a job and were often not taught any life skills or given any knowledge they could use on the outside world during their confinement. Meanwhile, voyeurs were paid hourly to scrutinize them, becoming dehumanized in the process.

In the last century a movement was born, and I was determined to nurture it to greater strength and power. The movement was called "Restorative Justice" (RJ).

RJ enables criminals to work out a proper restitution, make up the damage and try to compensate for, in some way, the harm they have caused, providing that the victims of their crimes were willing to accept the offer.

Seemed more civilized to me, and to a lot of other people also. It certainly seemed more practical. After all, helping one's fellow man get on the road to a productive life certainly paid off in higher multiples than keeping them in concrete enclosures. Seeing that they learned how to read, learned employable skills, made amends for the harm they had done, and were armed with the knowledge they needed to contribute to society, seemed only sensible.

It made the number crunchers happy too. Sure, there was and always will be the tiny percentage of people who are intractable. My middle name is not Pollyanna. We have habitable islands. The Rock is still there. Some individuals need to be restrained either for their own safety or for that of law-abiding citizens. That number is shrinking rapidly though.

Many former prison buildings now make almost impenetrable storehouses for non-perishables.

HISTORICAL NOTE:

The "Beautify America" campaign, which had been languishing due to lack of funds, was reinvigorated with just a fraction of the funding that had formerly gone to the upkeep of federal prison grounds.

X V

A Discordant Note

SADLY, SOME OF MY IDEAS never took off. The fifteen-hour music test law – a musician could only release a record after having listened to it themselves for 15 hours straight – never flew. Sabotaged by heavy opposition from freedom of speech advocates, although I had human rights activists on my side.

Then there was the elevator speaker replacement law, offering $10,000 to any company who manufactured those tinny elevator speakers to exchange them with human-friendly music systems. The idea flopped. Not one company owned up to having made the insulting sound boxes in the first place. Thankfully, digitizing seemed to handle that problem.

Another failure was the Gracious Waitress Law, requiring all service people to go through an apprenticeship somewhere in the Southeast to learn about real hospitality. Thwarted by some kind of anti-discrimination protest from a conclave of health food restaurant owners in Sedona. Still, it's funny how you tend to hear a hint of Virginia in restaurants all over the country these days.

The Get Green Law, requiring a proportionate amount of green space be created for every square foot of concrete constructed, also never saw the light of day. But at least I got funding for studies to show how people do much better in life-friendly spaces and the obstacles to building new complexes with no green complementary spaces just seem to get bigger and bigger.

My idea for a Computer Radius Law – free WIFI access, available to within a 2-mile radius of every single-family dwelling in the country – didn't cut it. Although non-profit groups did have an interesting method to their madness with which their donated computers stretched beyond schools and libraries, to hospital waiting rooms, post offices and even bus stops.

Being President does not mean you get everything you want ... well, not right away anyway.

XVI

I Digress

HOW I HATE THE WORD "normal." Marie Curry wasn't "normal." Helen Keller wasn't "normal." Einstein wasn't "normal." The Wright brothers weren't "normal." Abraham Lincoln wasn't "normal." Michael Jordan isn't "normal." Stephen Hawking wasn't "normal." And I'm just getting started.

How could any parent ever listen to some outsider try to tell them whether their child is normal or not? What are they measuring "normal" against?

And why, why, why, why, why would anybody want a "normal" child anyway?

Even worse, why would a parent ever give a child a drug to tune down those bright eyes, that active mind, and that unstoppable energy?

I will never understand it.

Lies spouted forth by many different sources are still the same lies. Fifteen syllable words to label child behavior – made up by people with fancy titles who have never been parents and somehow bypassed childhood themselves – are still gobbledygook.

Taking kids off sugar, showing them how to look up words in a dictionary, letting them run outside and play every three or four hours, getting them involved in dance, music, other arts does not make drug companies zillions of dollars; but it sure shows how amazing and original every single child can be when they are not turned into mindless automatons forced to robotically act like everyone else. I really do hate that word "normal."

Especially when it is applied to the billions of unique human beings on planet Earth.

Anyway, I digress, but I get to do that.

This, after all, is my book.

EPILOGUE

Those who comment on books will say this is not really an autobiography. True enough, as what you've just read omits key information, including:

- My name. (Wouldn't be fair to reveal before I even start training for the election marathon.)
- Contemplation of my days as a toddler.
- My most memorable meal.
- How I lost my virginity.

You have not even been given a full picture of my tenure.

You have read what I thought worth saying, with a hopefully interesting title. I mean, would anybody read a book entitled "Reflections by an Enlightened Female Word Leader on a New Direction for Earth in a Potentially Technocratic Future"?

I didn't think so either.

To a better future.

F.W.P.

www.ingramcontent.com/pod-product-compliance
Lightning Source LLC
Chambersburg PA
CBHW061044050726
47592CB00004B/1586

9780578617947